Needs
Past and Present

by Matthew Frank

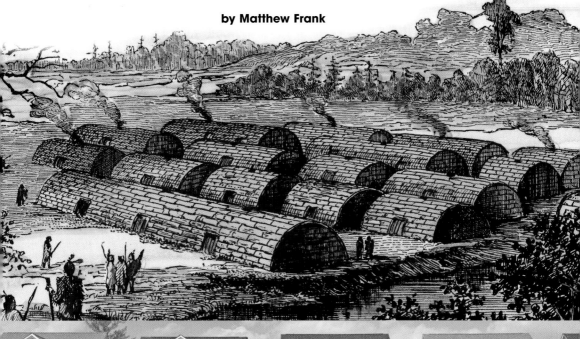

Table of Contents

Words to Think About

crops

People grow these crops for food.

Native Americans

Native Americans were the first Americans.

past

These Native Americans lived in the past (long ago).

present

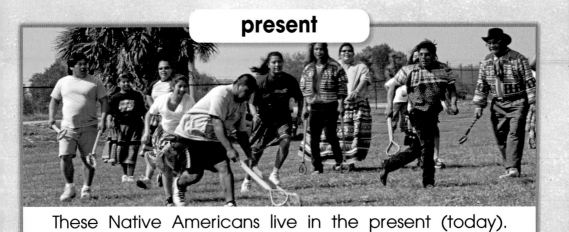

These Native Americans live in the present (today).

shelter

People had homes for shelter.

stores

Today we buy many things in stores.

Introduction

You need food, water, and clothing. You also need a place to live. People in the **past** had these needs, too.

food

water

Over time, the ways people meet their needs have changed. This book tells how. It compares people today with **Native Americans** long ago.

clothing

shelter

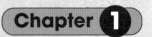

Chapter 1

Food

People need food to live. In the past, Native Americans hunted, caught fish, and grew **crops**.

▲ The Pueblo grew corn.

Food for Thought

The first crop was squash. People still grow squash today.

hunting

In the **present**, people eat many of the same foods that the Native Americans ate. But most people buy their food in **stores**.

▲ Today most of the food we buy and eat is grown on large farms.

crops

grocery store

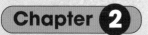

Chapter 2

Water

All living things need water. Long ago, many Native Americans got water from rivers and lakes.

▲ These Native Americans used water to cook.

Today most people have water in their homes. But the water still comes from rivers and lakes.

▲ Today people turn on a faucet to get water.

▲ Now many people buy water.

Chapter 3

Clothes

Clothes keep us warm and protect us from the hot sun. Long ago, Native Americans made their own clothes.

▲ Native Americans used materials they could make or find.

LOOK AT TEXT STRUCTURE

Compare and Contrast
The author uses the word "however" to show a contrast between the past and the present.

We wear clothes today, too. However, most of us buy our clothes in stores.

▲ Do you make your clothes, or do you shop for them?

Chapter 4

Shelter

People need **shelter** to stay safe. Each Native American group built homes from materials where they lived.

▲ The Lakota used buffalo hides to make tepees.

igloos

clay and straw adobe houses

Today builders make our homes. People live in apartments, houses, mobile homes, and houseboats.

▲ Homes are made of bricks, wood, and many other materials.

houseboats

mobile homes

Conclusion

Long ago, people needed food, water, clothing, and shelter.

Past

food

water

clothing

shelter

Today we still have these needs, but we meet them in different ways. How might people meet these needs in the future?

Present

food

water

clothing

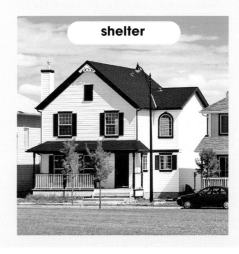

shelter

Glossary

crops plants that people use

See page 6.

Native Americans the first people to live in America

See page 5.

past time that has already happened

See page 4.

present time that is happening now

See page 7.

shelter a safe place to live

See page 12.

stores places where people buy and sell things

See page 7.

Index